One In A Million Faith

Saved By Grace

30 Days of Trusting God for the Impossible

Tamekia Green-Judge

DWilson & Associates, LLC

Copyright © 2021 DWilson & Associates, LLC
All rights reserved. Printed in the United States of America.
No part of this publication may be used or reproduced in any manner whatsoever without written permission from the publisher.

ISBN: 978-1-7366846-5-8

DEDICATION

I dedicate this devotional to my husband, James, and my son, Cameron. Thank you for loving and supporting me in everything I do.

MY PRAYER FOR YOU

I pray for the person who has opened this devotional to join me on this faith journey. May this walk be an experience like no other. May you be encouraged as you elevate your faith. May the true and living Father pour into you as you read, study, and believe you will be healed. May you be open to receive what God has for you.

I pray that God blesses you with faith that is one in a million. God's word declares in Hebrews 11:1, "Now faith is the substance of things hoped for, the evidence of things not seen."

I decree and declare your hope will be increased in things you could have only imagined. I pray you will believe in what you see and produce what you have only envisioned. Every doubt, every fear, every worry, every limited belief that has held you captive shall be destroyed. God, break the chains now. May God loose you from the strongholds that have caused you to hesitate and stopped you in the midst of your breakthrough. May our Heavenly Father give you hind feet to climb the mountains of life that seem impossible to climb.

I decree and declare that your faith will be activated to another level. For the Lord says in His word in Luke 1:37, "For with [Him] nothing shall be impossible." I decree and declare good health and breakthrough as you trust God and His word. During the times you move into uncharted territories, let the Holy Spirit rise, so that one-in-a-million faith may be deposited.

James 2:14 says, "What does it profit a man to have faith but no works?" I decree and declare that there will be evidence of one-in-a-million faith in action after the completion of this devotion.

Lord, I thank you for this life being transformed into new dimensions and deeper depths. I thank You knowing that when fear steps in, this reader will not lean on their own understanding but trust in You and move. For You are our Abba; You are our heavenly father, and You provide for your children. Now, God, activate Your child's faith and provide guidance on this journey for going deeper into the realm of faith with You. Lord, give Your child one-in-a-million faith.

In Jesus' name, I pray, amen.
- *Tamekia S. Green-Judge*

TABLE OF CONTENTS

FOREWORD

Introduction

Day 1 : The Way Maker 1

Day 2 : Trusting the Beholder 4

Day 3 : Unto Death, Or Not 8

Day 4 : Good Hope Through Grace 12

Day 5 : Grounded in Faith 16

Day 6 : Hope for the Hopeless 20

Day 7 : The Good Fight 24

Day 8 : Hold Fast, Don't Quit 28

Day 9 : The Master Plan 32

Day 10 : Perceiving the Glory of God 36

Day 11 : Sense of Hope 40

Day 12 : Unbelief is Fired 44

Day 13 : Because of Love 48

Day 14 : The Fire Starter 52

Day 15 : Blind Trust 56

Day 16 : Stay Focused 60

Day 17 : My Help 64

Day 18 : There Is Life in the Spirit 68

Day 19 : Out of God's Love 72

Day 20 : Christ Intercedes for Me 76

Day 21 : Change of Garment 80

Day 22 : Prosperity 84

Day 23 : Help Is On The Way 88

Day 24 : Gratitude 92

Day 25 : A Discerning Mind 96

Day 26 : Calling It Quits 100

Day 27 : The Lonely State 104

Day 28 : You Got The Victory 108

Day 29 : Refuge 112

Day 30 : Do Not Lose Heart 116

FOREWORD

R. Roberts, Apostle
Love House Ministries
Beaufort, S.C.

God has blessed me tremendously with a gifted CFO in Tamekia Judge. When she arrived in the ministry she was transitioning from religion to relationship with God. Her maturity was rapid and constant, with such an appetite for the things of God and ministry. Shortly, as she began to find her way and position in the Kingdom with an understanding of her spiritual identity, sickness came to challenge and perhaps even change the direction of her path.

In 2008, though Tamekia was young, energetic, full of life and filled with lofty goals, her life took a drastic change, a change that took her on a journey with more horrific twists and turns than an amusement ride. What would have easily caused others to put ministry on the shelf and focus solely on oneself and the health matter at hand, she stayed laboring in the vineyard. Ministry for her isn't something to put on a shelf like a decorative object or hang up like a garment; it is part of who she is and the calling that she answered from her heavenly father.

So, with sickness before her and family, work, and ministry pulling on her, what does she do? She takes them all on, not to mention that she was also in the midst of a graduate program, perfecting her professional craft. The most impressive thing is that to look at and interact with her, you would never know the pain and discomfort she was in because she wouldn't show it or say it. No, her fight would not be played out for all to see. It was for the select few who were willing to trust her God with her.

"One In A Million Faith" takes us on a journey of just one aspect of Tamekia's life stories. It helps us to not only understand her plight, but how to also find solace when possibly faced with life-threatening illnesses affecting us or a loved one. It is so clear that she isn't seeking the reader's sympathy; she is seeking to empower the reader to dare to take a journey of trust in the One who makes all things new, the God who heals and makes whole again.

This book will help you put life into perspective, to see how in a blink of an eye things can change, regardless of whether or not you are ready. We will not get a say about the timing or the severity of the change, but we do get to determine in whom we place our trust. The author helps us to know exactly where to look for our help and how to position ourselves to see the hand of God move.

Whether you're faced with catamenial pneumothorax and hemothorax or another condition found in medical journals, your faith will be tested and it is at that point, that moment, that intersection where life suddenly stops playing by the rules and compels you to make a decision. Will you cash it all in say your goodbyes, set your affairs in order and get casket ready? Or will you take a page from Tamekia's life and say, "I Shall Live and Not Die."

May God's healing hand rest upon you as you read this faith-building journey and determination of a woman who endured the sufferings of many physicians even those who left her for dead, yet found the courage and faith to touch the hem of Christ's garment to be made whole.

INTRODUCTION

"I shall live and not die"

Let's go on a journey to see what it is like to be a living witness to a miracle birthed by my faith in God. Walk with me and learn how you can overcome when you don't know whether you will live or die.

In 2008, my life as it was known suddenly changed. I was young, in my early thirties, healthier than ever, filled with life and energy. In fact, I was so healthy I did not take any medication or vitamins on a daily basis. Let me share with you how my life changed in the blink of an eye.

It all started in November 2008; I can remember it as if it were yesterday. I had gotten home from a long day at work and decided that I would relax, take a break, and ease my mind for a bit. I decided to sit on my bed and watch television. Watching a good cooking show always relaxes me. As I watched, the "Iron Chef" show, I started to feel discomfort as a pain started to well up in my chest. At first, the pain was dull, and then it became sharp, so I grabbed my chest and said to myself, "I know that I am not having a heart attack." At that moment, my heart started to beat faster, and the adrenalin began to pump because my heart was racing. Panic was beginning to rise up, right along with fear. I am not one who overreacts, so in order to avoid scaring my husband, I had not made him aware of what was taking place. By this time, I had somehow managed to ease myself onto the floor. As I sat on the floor, the pain was coming and going, almost similar to gas pains. That's when I became short of breath. What I noticed was that whenever I would try to take a deep breath, the pain worsened, and it was harder to breathe. I wanted to scream, but because I didn't want to alarm my husband, I allowed my stubbornness to make a decision: I did not go to the hospital or the doctor at that moment; that was crazy; don't ever allow flesh to speak louder than wisdom. I stretched out onto the floor in hopes that things would get better. After I had been there for a while, not sure exactly how long I was there, my husband came in and asked what had happened. The fear in his voice and the look in his eyes showed that he was worried; however, I felt better as the pain appeared to lessen. There remained, however, a bigger issue that was not easily visible.

You know fear will paralyze you and cause you to not move. I thought about what older people would have done, and that was to self-medicate until I could find something to ease the pain. My mind was telling me that it was something that I ate. I had no idea that my life was about to change forever. I had enough excitement for one night, so I ended up going to sleep.

About two weeks later, I was beginning to feel back to normal — healthy and energetic. I didn't have any pain. I was going to work, attending church services, and hanging out with my family and friends, enjoying life once again. I was at home relaxing, and a thought came to my mind that I should go to the doctor and get checked. Now, after I allowed that thought into my mind, I started having a gut feeling that something could be wrong, so I figured

I'd better go get checked out to be on the safe side. I contacted my physician to schedule an appointment; the office assistant who answered was very pleasant. I spoke with the young lady and briefly explained my concerns. Normally, it takes weeks to get in to see the doctor, but not this time. I was scheduled for a few days later, on a Friday, so I figured that I would go to work at the office after going to my appointment. It was a nice day out; the sun was shining, and there was a slight breeze blowing outside.

The pleasantness of the day could have not prepared me for what would happen, though. My plans would be turned upside down. I was thinking and hoping that I would have a routine checkup just to confirm that I was okay and that what I had experienced was only gas pains. I was feeling okay, so I did not have any concerns. I waited until the nurse called my name and escorted me to the exam room. The nurse checked my vitals and my temperature; we conversed cordially as I updated her on how my day was going. After the nurse stepped out of the room and as I waited for the doctor to enter, I started thinking about what I needed to get done when I arrived at work. There was a knock on the door, and the doctor entered. We chatted for a bit. Let me remind you, in my mind, this was just supposed to be a routine checkup because by this time the pain that I had felt in the previous weeks had disappeared.

My doctor is so sweet and compassionate. She began the exam by asking a series of questions -- you know, the usual: when did you begin to experience the pain; what were you doing when it all started, just so she would have a better understanding to determine a diagnosis. Then she started checking my eyes, ears -- the normal checkup. When my doctor prepared to listen to my breathing with the stethoscope, I made sure I was quiet so that she could hear well. The doctor placed the stethoscope on the left side of my back and said, "Take a deep breath in and let it out slowly." Then she switched to the right side and repeated the instructions, which I followed. While my doctor continued examining the right side as she was listening to my lungs, she asked, "Are you in any pain?" Now here is the scary part that actually got my attention. I'm wondering why she would ask me if I was in pain when I felt fine. There was a pause, and she asked me, "Are you feeling okay?"

I responded and said, "I feel okay. I have a little pain, but nothing that bad." Then the doctor said in a soft tone, "I don't want to worry you, but I need you to go to the emergency room to be checked out." My doctor was concerned because she was not able to hear any air flowing through my lungs on the right side. I became deer eyed and looked at her sideways, as if to say ... something is wrong with me.

My doctor, trying to be encouraging and assure me, said that there was nothing I should be worried about. She just wanted to determine what was going on with me. I started to feel a big lump form in my throat, and I believe at that moment I felt my blood pressure go up. The drive to the hospital's emergency room seemed like it took forever, as if I were driving in slow motion. Luckily for me, my doctor had called ahead to inform the emergency room staff of what she had observed and to inform them that I was on my way. When I arrived at the emergency room, the staff rushed me to the back. The doctor came in and spoke with me.

He pulled out his handy-dandy stethoscope and listened to my breathing, and he told me that I needed to have an x-ray performed. I went to the radiology department and was x-rayed, and then I went back to the exam room and waited on the results. It seemed like time had slowed down and my mind began to race yet again. My heart was feeling discouraged. That was fear trying to creep in because I didn't know the extent of what was taking place.

After what seemed like hours, the radiologist came into the exam room with the results. His concerned expression made my heart seem as though it skipped a beat. He shared the results with me, saying that the lung on the right side appeared to be collapsed and filled with fluid. By this time my eyes were bulging.

I was not prepared for what came out of his mouth next. I had to have a minor procedure (called thoracentesis) to remove the fluid so that my lung could fully re-expand and fill with air. My heart was beating so loudly I could hear it; if the doctor listened hard enough, he would have heard it too.

I was so grateful for the nurse who performed

the procedure prep, which consisted of placing a large needle through my back in order to draw out the fluid. The needle had to be at least five inches long. Never would I have imagined that two liters of fluid were in my lung. It took a couple days for the results to determined that the fluid was blood. It was on the inside of my lung, causing it to collapse and create all the pain that I was feeling on the inside of my chest. As soon as the fluid was drawn out, I felt something like a pop on the inside, and a couple hours later the lung re-expanded and I could breathe without the pain. I could breathe so well I felt like I could do back flips. I left the hospital and headed home. I spent that night consumed with thinking about what had taken place and wondering how it could have happened, because the doctors really didn't explain what caused my lung to fill with blood and collapse. I thought this was the fix to my issue, and I was good to go.

About two weeks later, while I was at home doing chores, I started having the chest pains again, and the shortness of breath followed. I said to myself, not again. To me, the pain seemed to be worse than before. I dropped everything that I was doing because the pain was unbearable. I went to the hospital emergency room, and lo and behold, I had to have another thoracentesis procedure.

Now the question was what was causing the reoccurring collapse and blood to fill my lungs? This time my lung didn't expand as quickly, so I had to spend the night at the hospital. My mind was all over the place. I felt heavy with the weight of the world, struggling to put the pieces together of this puzzle that was so confusing. Now I was really starting to think, because the doctors didn't have answers, and I had lots of questions. The main question was would I live or die? It's a scary feeling when you don't know what's happening; I couldn't see the big picture and wasn't able to get answers to the questions that had caused my mind to work overtime. I was at a place of desperation and in need of answers, quickly. I expected the doctors to know the answers, because they were the ones who went to school to study this stuff; not me, and yet, they had no idea what was ahead, and it hurt. My emotions were trying to get the best of me because none of the doctors could pinpoint what caused the issue.

I started to take matters into my own control. I had to figure this thing out, so, in order to assist the doctors, I had to monitor everything that I did daily to try to determine what was taking place. In January 2009, I began keeping a journal to track my routine and note what I was doing whenever the pain and shortness of breath started. I felt lost and helpless, with no direction at all. The main thing that I had to do was pray. As I prayed, I learned that I was taking on a matter that was outside of my control by a long shot. We often take matters into our hands as if God gave us control when He didn't.

I was referred to a lung specialist at the Medical University of South Carolina to try to figure out what was happening with my body. It would be another month before the next episode occurred. When it happened this time, I landed in the hospital in need of a chest tube. I remember it like it was yesterday. It was February 2010; my menstrual had arrived and along with it came chest pains and shortness of breath. When the pain hit, I was at work. I was working on processing permits, and all of a sudden, I started to get hot. I am usually cold, but I was so hot that I was sweating. So I thought, "Oh, boy, not again. This cannot keep happening."

It's a good thing that the hospital was only five minutes away from my job. I got to my car as fast as I could and drove straightway to the emergency room. I can't even tell you if I ran a red light or two getting there because everything seemed like a blur. The pain was so severe. At the emergency room, the doctor performed an x-ray, which showed my lungs collapsed and filled with blood. Then to make things worse, every time this happened, my iron levels would drop.

What became clear, though, thanks to my journaling, was that every time that my menstrual cycle would begin, my lungs would collapse and fill with blood. It was horrifying and nerve wracking because I knew that if something wasn't done about my issue, my lungs would collapse constantly with this repeated cycle. It seemed as though with each collapse, things became worse. This was very discouraging and draining on my body and my mind.

After meeting with several specialists at MUSC, Medical University of South Carolina, I learned that I needed surgery to stop my lung from collapsing and filling with fluid. My condition finally had a name: pneumothorax and hemothorax – which refers to the collapse of the lung and the air space filling with blood. I learned that I had a rare condition known as catamenial (which means related to the menstrual cycle) pneumothorax and hemothorax, and while I was relieved that we actually had a name for my condition, I was scared.

I felt that I was now a little closer to the root of the matter. The entire time that I was going through this ordeal, there wasn't much information out there because it was such a rare condition. Statistics showed that I was one in a million who would end up with such a disease. There was no known cure and really not much information about a cause. I had to endure several surgeries. After tests were completed on the samples earlier in the diagnosis, doctors determined that I had endometriosis in my lungs. This lung condition was related to my menstrual cycle, which now affected my ability to have more children; which created another issue.

Throughout this process, I had to stay in the light and not allow my mind to enter into the dark place called depression, which is a tool of the enemy. He wanted to take me out. When doctors couldn't help as I expected, it took everything that God had started working on within me for me not to give in to hopelessness and become downtrodden with unbelief as my faith was tested. Once you have seen the impossible made possible through prayer, something happens on the inside of you. Faith is birthed in your heart, and prayer takes on a fervency in your life. During this journey, God had to deliver me with not only healing, but also from myself. A place of bondage is where self-pity will take you when you are feeling alone without the ability to help yourself.

In February 2009, after surgery, I was hooked up to three large chest tubes to help my lungs inflate. At first, after I came out of surgery, I had one chest tube inserted. I watched the container continually fill with blood that came from my lung. The nurses and the doctors came in to examine me. I was taken to get x-rays done every several hours because the lung needed to be inflated. After I returned from getting an x-ray, the doctor told me they needed to add another chest tube. He said that the second one should help. Well, it didn't, and I ended up with another chest tube. As the third chest tube was inserted, my shoulders slumped over, and I sobbed because I needed my lungs to expand, and as I was crying, I reminded God of His words, that He said this would not take me out, and suddenly, peace fell over me like a blanket. Surely, if God restored breath and life in dead bones, He could restore the oxygen in my lungs so I could breathe again.

I stopped crying as I was sitting in the hospital bed. Several hours later, my lungs began to inflate. Now this was becoming overwhelming, and my emotional state had to be strengthened. As my thoughts were trying to get the best of me, I sat on the bed and started watching the chest tubes, and I decided that I should live and not die. I couldn't allow what I was seeing to break me. What caught my attention was that as I watched the fluids in the chest tubes change from blood to water, I was reminded of Jesus being on the cross as blood first came pouring out of His wounds and then came water. I heard in my Spirit, "Would you be a living sacrifice?" I started to cry because I was reminded of what Jesus went through on the cross and that I, too, had a cross to bear through this health battle. I shall live and not die. I said, "Yes, Lord, I will be a living sacrifice."

It was at that moment that I knew that I was going to make it. I was also reminded by the peace that I felt. God reminded me that this would not take me out. This is not a joyful battle when you look with the natural eyes. I had to remind myself that in the book of James, we must count it all joy when we are going through trials and tribulations. In order to overcome, you must be an overcomer with great faith, which is what was required during my journey.

It's a scary thing when you are believing in something you cannot see, yet knowing deep down that the outcome has to be better than what it seemed. Let's fast forward another year to 2010. I ended 2009 with a temporary chest tube that I kept for three months.

It was a Wednesday morning; I had not slept well. I tossed and turned all throughout the night, only to awake in pain, but not a lot. My breathing was labored, even with the chest tube. I had to get myself together, so I kept pressing and pushing myself as I ironed my clothes and showered, thinking that I would feel better after a hot shower. After I stepped out of the shower, I felt exhausted, worse than I did before I hopped in, but decided to keep getting ready for work. Sometimes my flesh causes me not to think straight. The older generation always spoke about their bodies giving us warning signals that we should pay attention to. I had no idea that the chest tube had stopped working, so I decided that I would go to work and remain hopeful that things would get better.

I was in for a surprise when I arrived to work. As I pulled into the parking lot, and jetted out of the car, and headed toward the building, and I suddenly felt as though I was having a heart attack. The breath that I had earlier seemed as though it had left my body. I staggered up the steps to the building, my heart racing a thousand miles a minute. When I got to my office, I thought I was going to die right there. Fear crept in like one could not imagine. After sitting at my desk for a while, I regained composure and was able to breathe. Then suddenly, I had an urge to use the restroom. Any other time I would not have hesitated, but because I was afraid, not knowing what would happen, I hesitated. Fear causes people to hesitate. It took several minutes before I finally made up in my mind to go to the restroom. I slowly walked down the hallway and was relieved when I made it there, as I was still feeling the heaviness in my chest. On my way back to the office, I lost the ability to breathe fully and I started gasping for air.

I made it to the office and saw my co-worker. She asked, "Are you okay?" I said, "No, I can't breathe," and as soon as those words came out of my mouth, my eyes began to fill with water. She then asked if she needed to call an ambulance. I told her no because it would take them too long to arrive. A car would be quicker. My co-worker grabbed her keys, and we headed to the emergency room. While I was there, the doctors came into the exam room and spoke with me about what I was experiencing. I had chest x-rays completed, and the nurse checked my temperature, which was now at 104 and climbing, I started to cough up blood.

My pastor had arrived at the emergency room, and I said to him, "I am going home from this place, but not to my heavenly home; I have too much to do." The doctor came in with the results of the x-ray. He explained that my lung was collapsed with a pneumothorax and a hemothorax and that my chest tube was not working properly, so he cleaned the tubes and had the nurse give me some ibuprofen. Then the doctor said he was sorry, but there wasn't really anything else that they could do for my situation.

I wondered what that meant. Did it mean they were sending me home to die? My ability to breathe had not restarted after the tubes were cleaned, and the chest tube was not removed. So, I looked at my pastor and I asked him what it all meant. I said, "I know they are not about to send me home without fixing the issue."

I started praying and I asked God, "What

am I supposed to do now?" As I waited on the discharge papers, my husband arrived. We left the emergency room, and I heard the Lord say to contact my doctor at MUSC, the Medical University of South Carolina. I thank God for the ability to hear and operate in obedience amid chaos and confusion. I had to remind myself to remember that because of God's grace and mercy, I was kept. He was with me when the doctors told me there was nothing more they could do for me. I remember my head starting to spin as I tried to wrap my mind around those words. The doctors gave me a pill and sent me on my way. Had I not been in a relationship with Christ, I don't believe that I would have been able to hear God, and I would not have contacted my doctor at MUSC. I probably would have gone home and accepted that there was nothing more that could be done for my condition.

I was stronger in my faith. No longer was I discouraged or fearful, and I was not going to allow life to end that way. I reminded God of what He had spoken. Sometimes it is good to remind God of His word in order to encourage yourself. This issue would no longer be a hindrance in my life. God is a God of order and so, I called my doctor and explained what took place. He contacted the doctors at the local hospital. I had to be taken to the medical university immediately, and an emergency surgery had to be performed on my lungs. The surgeon said that he had to remove a portion of my lung because it was covered with endometriosis. He had to attach my lung to the chest wall in order to help hold it up whenever it collapsed. I didn't know when the next time might have been, so my doctor did what he thought was best in order for me to be healed. I was encouraged by God's promise that I would live and not die, so I held on to the hope that no more collapse would occur. To this day, I have not had any reoccurrence of my lung collapsing. I thank God for answering my prayers and giving my doctor wisdom as God worked through him to care for me and not give up as others did.

ONE IN A MILLION FAITH | DAY 1

The Way Maker

"And the Lord, He is the One who goes before you; He will be with you; He will not leave you nor forsake you; do not fear nor be dismayed." (KJV)

DEUTERONOMY 31:8

The Lord goes before us even in the midst of our issues, trials, and tribulations. On the day that I was sitting in the doctor's office and was told that I needed to go to the emergency room because my doctor was unable to hear any air passing through my lungs, I became discouraged. If God had not gone before me, I would not have been prepared for what was about to happen in my life. God is the Alpha and the Omega, the beginning and the end, and He knows all things. Who would have known that I would be healthy one day — a busy multifaceted individual — and down the next day? When God goes before us, He paves the way by positioning people who are connected to the assignment, preparing our hearts and minds to align with His plan. Oftentimes when we are faced with a health crisis, we don't know the next step to take. With Jehovah Rapha, we have the crooked paths straightened because the Healer has gone before us, moving the stumbling blocks and the hindrances that the enemy has set up. The right people are in place, with the right words

ONE IN A MILLION FAITH | DAY 1

to speak into your life. The Holy Spirit guides in the midst of our fears. When you don't know what lies ahead, the enemy will come to bring fear to stop you in your tracks. Remember, I was healthy as a horse and got stopped for a moment with the blow of the news, "You need to go to the emergency room." We must trust the plan of God without fearing the unknown, regardless of what the doctors say.

Heavenly Father, thank you for going before us in all things, paving the way for the plans and purposes of our life. Thank you for never leaving nor forsaking us as you make the crooked paths straight.

Question: Are you allowing the Holy Spirit to guide you through the crisis? What do you need to do to shift so God is leading the way?

ONE IN A MILLION FAITH | DAY 2

Trusting the Beholder

"And those who know your name put their trust in you, for you, O Lord, have not forsaken those who seek you." (KJV)

PSALM 9:10

When we put our trust in God, He watches out for us. When we put our confidence in God, He smiles upon us with His favor. David put his faith in God. I put my trust in God to deliver and heal me. I went to church, and it was time for altar call, so I decided to get into the line for prayer for healing. The pastor connected in prayer with me for total healing of my body. At this time, I was already on surgery number three. When you think about the number of surgeries I had gone through, it was a little hard to say trust when I couldn't see the results of healing. Somehow, it was different this time. When the pastor prayed, the Lord began to speak, and I heard, "This will not take you out." I had reached a point where I couldn't trust what the doctors were saying because it was one surgery after another, still with no known cause for this rare disease. Because of this, I had to trust God to deliver and heal me. I had to allow those words to become rooted in my spirit and hold on to those words, reminding myself that the Lord is faithful to deliver, that He is not a man who will lie. His words never return to Him void; therefore, I must be healed. I shall be restored. God's words began to speak louder than any other words that I have heard since the beginning of my illness. God's words spoke louder than the fear that the enemy tried to place upon me. The Beholder, Jehovah, hid me in His bosom, to shield, protect and allow me to feel his love. When you know that you are loved, you will trust. In life we experience a variety of circumstances and issues, and it is crucial for us to trust God. According to God's promise, I was coming out of the house of affliction and into the plans of God healing my body, not being in bondage to sickness.

Father, thank You for placing your trust and confidence within me. As I seek your face for wisdom and direction, I will trust You.

Question: Are you seeking God with confidence? In which areas do you need to trust Him more?

ONE IN A MILLION FAITH | DAY 3

Unto Death, Or Not

"For indeed he was sick nigh until death: but God had mercy on him; and not on him only, but on me also, lest I should have sorrow upon sorrow." (KJV)

PHILIPPIANS 2:27

Our Father is merciful and compassionate when it comes to his children. No matter what we are faced with, God's mercies are renewed each and every day. My rare disease caused me to feel helpless, and I began to doubt my God, who is a healer. God is the one whom we serve in spirit and in truth. As my health appeared to worsen, God showed His mercy upon me each and every day that He allowed me to live for yet another moment. At this point, I was on surgery number four, with little to no understanding of why I had to be the one in a million chosen to go through this ordeal.

ONE IN A MILLION FAITH | DAY 3

Father, thank You for having the final say. No man knows the day nor the hour. Thank You for perfect timing.

Question: Are you willing to be the living sacrifice? How can you do that in your daily walk with Him?

ONE IN A MILLION FAITH | DAY 4

Good Hope Through Grace

"Now our Lord Jesus Christ himself, and God, even our Father, which hath loved us, and hath given us everlasting consolation and good hope through grace" (KJV)

II THESSALONIANS 2:16

God's grace is sufficient. We are not worthy of grace; however, God willingly gives it to us. I am one thankful woman because of God's grace. The hope that I received after bouts of depression, not knowing whether I would live or die, did something to my soul. The Messiah gives understanding and wisdom as you trust Him on this journey. When the enemy comes to attack your mind, God's grace is there to help you get back into the Word, drawing near to God. We mess up by complaining when we don't understand what is taking place in our lives. God's grace is there to pick you up. Our Lord and Savior is faithful even in our dark places. Being sick sometimes will take you to a dark place called depression. This is when your emotions become greater than reality. Throughout my stints in the hospital, the enemy came several times to make me doubt what God had spoken. I remember while I was in the hospital, I had just had an emergency surgery and had two chest tubes inserted to inflate my lungs, and it did not appear that my lungs would inflate, so the doctor brought in yet another chest tube. My hope had dropped as though things weren't going to improve. Yet, because of God's grace, my mind was not overtaken with doubt, but my faith started increasing as I believed that my lungs would, in fact, inflate. The grace of God changed my perspective. The light at the end of this tunnel was starting to brighten. I was no longer in darkness, giving glory to the enemy, but giving glory to the true and living God. When you deal with loss of hope, you are robbed of your peace. Where the Spirit of the Lord is there are liberty and freedom. Because of God's grace, my portion was a peace that surpasses all understanding.

Father, thank you for supplying grace that is sufficient. Because of the Father's grace, we receive God's mercy. We shall make it even though we may not understand. With our lack of understanding, we will hold fast to your Word.

Question: Will you allow the greater hope to rise, to overcome?

ONE IN A MILLION FAITH | DAY 5

Grounded in Faith

"If ye continue in the faith grounded and settled, and be not moved away from the hope of the gospel, which ye have heard, and which was preached to every creature which is under heaven; whereof I, Paul, am made a minister." (KJV)

COLOSSIANS 1:23

*I*n society, there are a lot of people who are not settled in their spirits or grounded in faith. Many allow life trials and tribulations to uproot their faith, and they begin to settle for less. I was one of these people. I had to make a decision that my rare condition would not destroy my faith in a God, whom I have known to be a miracle worker and an ultimate healer. He is the giver of life, and it is not His position to decommission someone for being ill. As I lay in the hospital bed, I started to question God, asking why I had to be the one to go through this, surgery after surgery after surgery with no sight of healing. We serve a mighty God who began a good work within us and continues the good work even on our sick beds. I knew that God didn't make mistakes and all things served a purpose, so I continued to hold on to the faith for a healing that I had to speak into existence as I trusted God, because I wasn't able to see it naturally. When the words "I shall live and not die" came forth, they became active. This in turn ignited my faith as God continued the work that He had already

ONE IN A MILLION FAITH | DAY 5

begun within me. I had to decree and declare some things into the atmosphere, and I prayed to move the heart of God in faith and not just by His hands. Healing is the children's bread, and as a child of God, I knew deep down on the inside that God was working out a plan to heal me. What I did not know is that He required me to be a living sacrifice. When others see you staying strong, believing God for a miracle, trusting God for healing, their faith is ignited. It's almost like a baby leaping inside you. When a person's faith is dwindling and they see you what you've overcome -- or better yet, what you are still dealing with, spirit to spirit, faith to faith -- a spark of ignition takes control, and they see God's ministering to those even while on their sick beds, and this increases their faith.

God, I thank you for who You are and all You do to settle our spirits. Thank You for rooting us in Your Word that we may have strength to go through all that we face. Because of your Holy Spirit, we shall be led along the straight path, where we meet victory at the end.

Question: What decision will you make?

ONE IN A MILLION FAITH | DAY 6

Hope for the Hopeless

"And we desire that every one of you do shew the same diligence to the full assurance of hope unto the end." (KJV)

HEBREWS **6:11**

According to Hebrews 11:1, "Faith is the substance of things hoped for and the evidence of things unseen." I used to say all the time as I was growing up, if I don't have anything else, I have hope. That was tested during another one of my episodes and stays in the hospital. There are twelve months in a year. Out of the twelve months in that particular year, I spent time in the hospital at least nine of those months. My overall illness, from diagnosis to healing, was about a five-year process. That was enough time for my faith to seesaw and for my hope to come and go. When you begin thinking of all the things that had taken place thus far, I had to be reminded of the Hope of God. The Lord gives full assurance until the end. If you allow your hope and your faith to be quickened and strengthened, what you are faced with will seem minimal. Understanding that Jehovah, Emmanuel will give hope to the hopeless and strength to the weak, then we can make it. I had to hold on to what I could not see, trusting and believing in a God to heal my body, mind, and soul.

ONE IN A MILLION FAITH | DAY 6

I am thankful for God's grace, because through the midst of all I was faced with, I was sure that the enemy would win. Not so! God said that we are victorious. God delivered and healed the woman who dealt with the issue of blood for over twelve years, so surely my five-year crisis was nothing. I felt as the woman did; I thought I was never going to be healed. The enemy tried to make me think that each time my menstrual cycle started and my lungs collapsed and filled with blood, that it was the end, trying to cause my hope and faith to be tainted. But God! I started reading scriptures on faith, and I studied the book of Jeremiah. Healing belonged to me. By doing so, my hope and my faith began to rise to another level. I could see again. I could believe with a greater faith. I will live and not die.

Thank you, Father, for your amazing power and work in my life. Thank you for your goodness and blessings over me. Thank you that you are able to bring hope through even the toughest times, strengthening me for a greater purpose. Thank you for elevation of faith through the midst of the affliction, trials, and tribulation.

Question: Are you willing to endure until the end?

ONE IN A MILLION FAITH | DAY 7

The Good Fight

"Fight the good fight of faith, lay hold on eternal life, whereunto thou art also called, and hast professed a good profession before many witnesses." (KJV)

I TIMOTHY 6:12

My mission is to help those who have lost faith, who have lost hope because of the challenges they face with illnesses, various diseases, trials, and tribulations that tried to overtake them. I want to encourage you all to know that God has the final say with our lives and when the appointed time shall be. Fighting the good fight will require having confidence in God, having trust and having faith beyond what you see in the natural world. When you persevere through the "I can't" or the "I'm sorry," and even the testing, know that God is your strength.

1 Corinthians 2:3 states, "And I was with you in weakness, and in fear, and in much trembling." God is with us no matter what or where we may be. As I lay on the operating table, My Lord was with me to bring me through and out of the surgery victoriously. After one of my surgeries, it took about three additional hours for me to recover and wake up. That was by the grace of God calling my name and telling me to continue the fight. The Holy Spirit speaks in many different ways. What I learned throughout this process is that I wasn't fighting alone. My family and your families get a chance to draw closer to God as we fight together for life. My family's love grew

as did their faith in what God was working out on my behalf. They were not only witnesses but partakers of the fruit that was produced as they saw the miracle. I had survived and was able to live when man said that I wasn't going to make it. Understand that the fight is because the enemy is trying to steal your faith. You must recognize what the enemy is trying to do, recognize that the battleground is in the mind. One must recognize the weapons of victory as the word of God. Throughout my illness, I continually confessed the word of God over my life. Decreeing and declaring that I was healed and that victory over sickness belonged to me. As you confess the word of God, it builds up your faith. Always remember, your mind is the workshop where the product and the materials of the enemy try to fill your mind. Know this: your mind is the mind of Christ, who builds the faith within you.

Father, I thank you for your incredible sacrifice so that I might have freedom and life. So many times, when I find myself in the pit of despair, I fight in my own strength, and by now, I know that it doesn't work. Help me to look to You at all times. You stand ready to help me when I seek your face daily.

Question: What happens when it seems like you are losing the fight?

ONE IN A MILLION FAITH | DAY 8

Hold Fast, Don't Quit

"Now faith is the substance of things hoped for, the evidence of things not seen. For by it the elders obtained a good report." (KJV)

HEBREW 11:1-2

On this journey of sickness, one thing that I learned was that you must hold fast to your faith. It is important because the enemy comes to fight you because of where you are going. People suffer sicknesses, diseases, and other illnesses for various reasons that are often out of our control. Holding fast to your unseen victory is a must. Quitting is not an option just because you can't see the end results. As you allow God's healing virtue to flow through your body and manifest healing, you will receive the good report in the end. If I had allowed myself to hold on to the words spoken by the doctors telling me "There is nothing else that we can do for you," I would have allowed myself to believe the report of man and worst of all, I would have probably quit, or worse yet, died. I always tell people if it had not been for a relationship with Christ, I would not have had enough sustenance to hold on. In our flesh, it is our human nature to settle at times when things are out of our control, especially if you don't understand whose you are. Our Father empowers us to hold on and press forward.

ONE IN A MILLION FAITH | DAY 8

Always remind yourself of the importance of holding on tight to God's hand as we trust and believe the truth of God's word.

Father, as my steps are ordered by you throughout the journey, I want to thank you for the ability to hold fast to the faith that you instill within me as I hold on to your healing hands. If it had not been for your virtue, I would not be able to share my testimony. Father, you empowered me to trust and receive a good report.

Question: Ask yourself, whose report will you believe?

ONE IN A MILLION FAITH | DAY 9

The Master Plan

"For I know the thoughts that I think toward you, saith the Lord, thoughts of peace, and not of evil, to give you an expected end." (KJV)

JEREMIAH 29:11

Jehovah is a God who makes plans according to His will and His purpose. Because we are human, it is in our nature to plan how we want things to be; however, in the end God's plans shall prevail. When the storm of life hits, we must be ready; however, we hardly ever plan for the what ifs in every situation. When life is going well or appears to be in line with the plans that we created, when an illness disrupts the alignment, the straight paths have now become temporarily crooked. Our Lord and Savior makes the crooked paths straight according to His will. According to God's promise I was going to come out of the house of affliction and into the plans of God healing my body, not being in bondage to sickness any longer. However, this did not happen overnight. I had to endure a series of surgeries to get to the plan that God had -- the plan of trusting, the plan of greater faith, the plan of victory, and best of all was the assignment. When you say "Yes" to God, you must have an expectancy that life now has to be yielded for the greater good. This is easier said

ONE IN A MILLION FAITH | DAY 9

than done. With each of my hospital stays, and with my not knowing how long I would have to endure the pain and fear, the enemy came to rob me of my peace in every way. When you don't have peace, it doesn't mean that the Father is not with you, because He is; He is Emmanuel. A reminder that God is in control of the things that happen to reassures us of His peace. Jehovah Shalom, the Prince of Peace, gives the peace that surpasses understanding as we accept His plans for our life, even with the storms that create a detour.

God's response to many questions that we have are "Yes" and "Amen." Understanding the power of "yes" helped me to receive the victory in the end. Thank you, Father, for the "Yes" that saved my life. Because you went before the Almighty on my behalf with Your "yes," I live.

Question: Are you willing to accept the plans that God has created?

ONE IN A MILLION FAITH | DAY 10

Perceiving the Glory of God

"When Jesus heard that, he said, this sickness is not unto death, but for the glory of God, that the Son of God might be glorified thereby." (KJV)

JOHN 11:4

𝓕aith is a necessity on this journey. As Mary and Martha knew in their heart that Lazarus was presumed dead, he was not dead in the heart of Jesus. This is what happens with many of us when we look through the natural eyes and not with our spiritual eyes. What appeared to be dead was full of life. In today's world, whenever a person is diagnosed with a life-threatening illness, people are more oft to put a time limit on the individual's life. In my case, the doctors tried to do the same, except the greater God whom I serve is the only one who knows the appointed time for eternity. Everything that is done is for the glory of God, that the Son of God may be glorified. The faith that is rooted within us sometimes needs a quickening or a revival to become active. The word of God states, "Faith without works is dead." For you to have active faith, the word of God must be the tool in your pockets, or better yet, in your heart. Your situation may look impossible; it may seem some things are dead and buried, but God says to rouse up your faith and look with eyes on Him, for this is not a situ-

ONE IN A MILLION FAITH | DAY 10

ation unto death, but unto His glory! Just as my health report appeared to be unto death, those dead dreams, those lost souls, the bad breaks – those situations and every situation that looks dead and buried should all be used to glorify God as new life is started. Romans 8:28, "And we know that all things work together for the good to them that love God, to them who are the called according to His purpose. No matter what we are faced with, God keeps those He wants for His purpose on purpose.

Thank you, Father, for being in control of my life. You have filled me with the mind of Christ, faith, and the strength to fight to live. I know that You have my back and that You brought me out of the bed of affliction. My Lord, Your love for me lifted me out of the bed and restored my health. Thank you for complete restoration.

Question: When sickness comes to take you out, you are given the choice to give up or to fight. What are you willing to fight for?

ONE IN A MILLION FAITH | DAY 11

Sense of Hope

"And thou shalt be secure, because there is hope." (KJV)

JOB 11:18

When you have been through a lot, God gives life, a sense of hope that says He hasn't forgotten about you. He's sending help. He's entrusting you with one of His precious gifts to bring about hope, love, and joy. He gives restoration that brings bonding and mending of relationships. Love covers over a multitude of sins. With the love that God sent, hearts are mended as relationships are restored. The addition brings about a change of focus and a new thought process that show how mighty God is and that He works in mysterious ways. When God restores, God heals that which was broken. The process of closing the hole has begun; now it's smaller than before. Keep hoping, believing, and trusting God in faith. The best is yet to come, because God is the holder of the keys for the master plan He has prepared for us. We will not allow the storms that come our way to stop our hope.

ONE IN A MILLION FAITH | DAY 11

Father, I thank you that your promises are true and that you make all things work for my good. When I don't understand what's going on, I still choose to have hope in you. You are faithful, and your promises are renewed everyday. You did not tell us we would live without trials, but you do promise to be our refuge and strong tower we can run into.

Question: Trusting God provides security. What are you allowing to block the security of hope?

ONE IN A MILLION FAITH | DAY 12

Unbelief is Fired

"For God hath concluded them in all unbelief, that He might have mercy upon all." (KJV)

ROMANS 11:32

In this season, beliefs have to be restored and unbelief denounced. The season of faith and trust is now. Trying to move through life's trials and tribulations requires a belief system in the most high God. Our beliefs are achieved by our faith in God. The beliefs must be rooted, because our faith is the substance of things hoped for and the evidence of things unseen. This creates a greater trust in God. The roots of unbelief begin when we start to doubt or question what God is speaking to our spirit man. We often question God when we don't understand. When this happens, we open a door for the enemy to come in and he in turn causes us to doubt the things that we know to be true of God. Unbelief causes a distance between us and God. With belief, we believe God and have the door open to a testimony of the things God has done in our life, the healing, the deliverance, the miracles, the blessings -- so many things that God does because He loves us. This is why it is important to guard our hearts and our minds. As believers, we know that Christ dwells in us. For greater

ONE IN A MILLION FAITH | DAY 12

is He that is in us than He that is in the world. Our hearts lead us away from the living God when we stubbornly refuse to believe in Him and obey. Our heavenly Father loves us so much that He doesn't want us to suffer, but when we do, His Holy Spirit is there to comfort us as He strengthens us. Faith building is a requirement in this journey. Belief is built from faith, so get this tool in your heart; it is a weapon of our warfare.

Father, I thank you for removing my unbelief. You did not allow a spiritual separation from You, but you drew me closer to you, so that you are glorified. Thank you for equipping me with the full armor and providing the tools that are used to fight when the doubt tries to rise. Lord, You are a hedge of protection, and You cover my mind from all unbelief.

Question: What tools are you using to combat unbelief?

ONE IN A MILLION FAITH | DAY 13

Because of Love

"And shewing mercy unto thousands of them that love me, and keep my commandments." (KJV)

EXODUS 20:6

We serve a merciful and loving God. When we operate in obedience and follow the commandments of God, it pleases Him. One of the names our Father is known as is love. There is no greater love than the love of God. We must always walk in love. As the word of God instructs, we must love the Lord Our God with all our hearts. Continue walking in His love. As we move along this journey called life, we must let the LOVE THING be our first response to every disappointment and every challenge. So many of us have faced challenges that tested or tried our faith and our love for God. Oftentimes when life is not filled with excitement, but filled with one problem after another, the heart starts to grow a little cold. Refuse to allow resentment to enter in to your emotions because of the trials and circumstances you sometimes face. Reject all bitterness and self-hatred. You are accepted in the beloved. You are the apple of God's eye. His love and care over you is unfailing and constant at all times. Keep a purpose to press into the righteousness, peace, and joy that is God's kingdom. Jehovah will bring you to the place where everything you say and do becomes as effective as if He said it or did it. Let God's peace act as the umpire in your heart, settling with finality every controversy, every expectation. The love of God is so powerful, it heals our hurts, our pain, and our sicknesses. In the ministry that I am a member of, several of the members use the phrase, "I will love you to life" instead of "I will love you to death" mainly because they understand that love heals and gives life. Love also pleases God. Allow the love of Abba Father to penetrate your hearts so that you can be healed, physically, mentally, and spiritually. Fear not but believe only and you will see of the travail of your soul and be satisfied.

Father, You are the love that took on death on the cross so that I may live. As You saturated me with your presence, your love surrounded me, and I know that you were continuing the work within me and allowed your mercy to manifest, so that I would recognize my healing.

Question: What is stopping you from loving fully?

ONE IN A MILLION FAITH | DAY 14

The Fire Starter

"The tongue also is a fire, a world of evil among the parts of the body. It corrupts the whole person, sets the whole course of his life on fire, and is itself set on fire by hell."
(KJV)

JAMES 3:6

Though the tongue is small, it can build an enormous fire with our words, so we must be careful. Many people don't understand or recognize the power of their words. Don't enter the gates with complaining, but enter the gates with praise and thanksgiving. Worship God as you enter the gates so He can move on your behalf. You can't speak with a double tongue, speaking curses and blessings at the same time, because the words shall not be honored. Oftentimes we become like the children of Israel when they were going through the wilderness. Depending on our state of mind, our circumstance, or our situation, we, too, are as in the place of wilderness. My illness started to turn into my phase of wilderness because I did not have a sudden healing. I had to deal with the affliction for several years before total healing was manifested. If you are in a state of weakness, hurt or pain, you want things done instantly. You want your finances fixed; you want your marriage restored; you want your child to return home, and as our human nature influences us, the first thing we often do is complain. We allow the little pink muscle to have its way. I

ONE IN A MILLION FAITH | DAY 14

wanted to be healed but because it seemed like it was taking forever; I started to complain about the hospital and all that's within instead of thanking God for healing despite it all, asking God for wisdom for those doctors who were about to treat me. I complained, creating an atmosphere of chaos and turmoil instead of an atmosphere that welcomed the Holy Spirit to move as He needed in order to bring results that let the people know that He is God, Jehovah-Rapha. The power of the tongue speaks life or death. The power of the tongue places limitations. The power of the tongue causes us to give glory to the enemy, when all glory belongs to the Father. We must ask God to tame our tongues as we go through trials and tribulations so that God can be the healer in our lives.

Lord, thank you for empowering me to tame my tongue and deliver me from the spirit of self-destruction. Father, as you change my speech from negative to one of positive encouragement, I thank You that I will no longer complain for lack of understanding. Because of You, I have the ability to speak your word into the atmosphere and change it to one that aligns with Your word, and I will be healed.

Question: Why do we allow something so small to have so much power in our life?

Blind Trust

"The God of my rock, in Him will I trust."
(KJV)

II Samuel 22:3

No matter what we are faced with or what we go through, there must be a level of trust in someone or something. True believers must have a level of trust in God to believe Him to answer your prayers. There cannot be a shared responsibility with doubt. Trust looms to receive the things asked for, and it comes. Trust is not a belief that God can or will bless; it is knowing that He does bless. God can do the impossible. Trust operates in present tense while hope looks at the future because of expectations. Trust possesses. So, when you pray, trust GOD at all times. There must be a connection between faith and trust in order for trust to be ignited, and for the hand of God to move on your behalf. When we trust God, we are not moving in our own strength or our own will. As we rely solely on the rock of God, the solid foundation to move within our lives when we are up and when we are down, we have given the sovereign God full control to do as He pleases. We must be willing vessels that yield to the will of the Holy Spirit. As you go through the demands of life, some

ONE IN A MILLION FAITH | DAY 15

things we trust God with, and others we take control of, as to say, "God, we can handle this situation better," knowing that we cannot. I remember there was a time when I was trying to self-diagnose instead of listening to the wisdom of the doctor, and it did not turn out so well and resulted in another stay in the hospital. Never take matters in your own hands unless God has given you the skills and the ability to handle the situation. Put all of your trust in God and not in man; the results will be much better.

Father, thank You for being my solid rock that gives me stability as I am going through this sickness. As you lift me up, I won't give up. As You remove the rocks of the enemy and You make every crooked path straight, so that healing comes forth.

Question: As we go through life, it will seem as though life is throwing rocks at us as we live for Jesus. We cannot allow the rocks to knock us out no matter what we are faced with. God is our rock that helps us to stand. Which rock are you allowing to take precedence?

Stay Focused

"Clothe yourselves with the full armor of God so that you may be able to stand against the schemes of the devil." (KJV)

EPHESIANS 6:11

Scripture tells us that we should put on the full armor or God so that we can stand against the schemes of the devil. It is the enemy's job to capture our attention and distract us from the things of the Father. When we are dealing with the turmoil of life, we really must remain focused. The Father says today, keep the main thing the main thing. Refuse to be distracted by the pressures around you. Incline your ear to God's still, small voice. Learn to ask the right questions at the right time. This is where listening and focus are important. There were many times that I went to the doctor, and couldn't remember everything that was said because I was so focused on the illness. That's enough to consume the thought process. There are times that we are not getting the right answers because we aren't asking the right questions. The Messiah delights in walking with us into circumstances and situations that will bring many questions to light as to what to do next. Never assume that the obvious solution to the problem we face at any given moment is what we should be asking God

ONE IN A MILLION FAITH | DAY 16

to do. Distractions must be removed because we must learn not to pray the process, but the outcome. Don't put your faith or focus your prayers on how you think the problem gripping your life right now will get solved. How you think things should go will seldom reflect what God actually has planned. God will remove the distractions, the stumbling blocks, and the issues of life as we release our will unto Him. God will help us to stand against the evil and the deceptions of the enemy when he comes to distract us. The word of God reads in Isaiah 59:19, "When the enemy shall come in like a flood, the Spirit of the Lord shall lift up a standard against him." The issues of life along with the burdens that impact us will not keep us down, because the full armor of God is there to help us stand.

Father, thank You for designing me to escape the whirlwind that came to destroy my life. You equipped me with the full armor to stand and to win. Thank You, Lord, for the victory of overcoming the battles that I am facing.

Question: The full armor of God equips us. When the whirlwind of life comes, will your armor stand?

ONE IN A MILLION FAITH | DAY 17

My Help

"But they that wait upon the Lord shall renew their strength; they shall mount up with wings as eagles; they shall run, and not be weary; and they shall walk, and not faint." (KJV)

Isaiah 40: 31

God's timing is the right timing. As we wait on God, He will renew our strength and bring us out of the place of despair, healing us of the infirmities, the sickness, the pain, and what seems like suffering. The affliction that was placed upon you and me serve purpose. We are overcome by the grace that is poured out upon us. Though we are not worthy, God allows us to be kept that He may get the glory. As we look to the hills from where our help comes from, Adoni speaks so that we are delivered and redeemed from the stronghold of sickness and disease. We shall conquer the illnesses that come to steal our joy, rob us of our peace. God came so that we may live and not die. We shall overcome everything that doesn't align with the will of God's plan. The enemy is rendered powerless. In Isaiah 58:9 the call for help begins, "Then shalt thou call, and the Lord shall answer; thou shalt cry, and He shall say, Here I am. If thou take away from the midst of thee the yoke, the putting forth of the finger, and speaking vanity." As we cry out, our tears are the call to our Lord for help. God hears the cries of His people and He moves upon us to heal, be delivered, and set free. No longer shall we be helpless in our

ONE IN A MILLION FAITH | DAY 17

circumstances or in our afflictions. Even in our downfall, God is there to help restore, revive, lift up, heal, strengthen, and set us free. As I ventured through this journey, my patience was tried over and over until it seemed like I was not going to make it. As I waited on God and as I waited on answers from the doctors' test results to come in, everything took time. Nothing was instant. I grew to have patience. I had gained the ability to value time as I waited. I drew closer to God because it gave me more time to pray, study, and read the Word of God. It also allowed me to share my God with others as I waited. I understood that my healing would take place in God's timing. One day is a thousand years to God, so if He wanted a microwave healing to come forth, he would have done so. It was a process; it was an assignment that would not be completed without God.

Father, I give my situation over to You and I surrender and submit my will and my timing to wait on You to show me what the next step is in your plan. As you remove yoke of sickness, I declare that this affliction will be removed as You keep me safe from the hands of death. I trust that You will see me through.

Question: In the right timing, many things take place; are you willing to wait on God's timing?

ONE IN A MILLION FAITH | DAY 18

There Is Life in the Spirit

"If the Spirit of Him who raised Jesus from the dead dwells in you, He who raised Christ Jesus from the dead will also give life to your mortal bodies through His Spirit who dwells in you." (ESV)

ROMANS 8:11

Everything that God created is good. Creation was done is such a wonderful way that the only purpose of His creations is to glorify God. The characteristics instilled within us, which make us in the image of Christ, will allow others to see, learn, and to know who God is when the burdens of life strike. The true and the living God shall make unbelievers tremble at the knowledge of Him. Miracles, signs, and wonders occur because of the Spirit of God being within us. God shows the unbelievers that He is God and that He has the power to do anything but fail. When you have the Spirit of God within you, you are not operating in self. The flesh is fully surrendered over to Christ. When we ask God to heal our bodies and we profess the words of faith over ourselves, we must trust that the giver of life will heal. As I lay in the hospital bed, my mind raced with so many thoughts that were beyond my control. As I continued to lift God up high, He reminded me that the Great I Am was within me. He was in control. It is human nature to take control of matters that we cannot fix.

ONE IN A MILLION FAITH | DAY 18

When this happens it slows the process because we need God to get us through the situation, and in this case, I needed to be healed and could not do it on my own. I had to rely on the Spirit of God, the power of God, and the strength of God to bring me through. As Jesus raised the little girl from her death bed, He gives life to our mortal bodies as well. God brings freedom from the slavery of a sickness. We are not to be overcome by the disease, affliction, or sicknesses that comes to attach itself; we are the overcomer.

Father, thank you for performing a miracle in my life. You are the Almighty Father to whom I surrender my will as You allow your Holy Spirit to dwell within me. You redeemed me so that I was not overcome by a rare disease that had no authority over me.

Question: What will you allow the Spirit of the Lord to help you overcome?

ONE IN A MILLION FAITH | DAY 19

Out of God's Love

"For God so loved the world, that he gave His only Son, that whoever believes in Him should not perish but have eternal life."
(KJV)

JOHN 3:16

Out of God's love, He gave up his only begoten son, Jesus Christ, so that He could stand in our place and take all of the consequences for the sin we were born into. It is not every day that someone takes our place when we are faced with trials and tribulations, sicknesses and turmoil. Many would say, "I will pray for you and leave you to be." But God, the lover of our souls, gave His only begotten son. The God we serve is awesome: It was His love that compelled Jesus to heal those who were struck down by infirmities and lifelong ailments. Look at the woman with the issue of blood: The virtue healed her because of her faith. There was the lame man in the pool of Bethesda who was healed because of the love and faith that resonated within him. For many, it seemed like an eternal sickness, or worse yet, sickness unto death was going to overtake them. I am a living testament of God's love and the miracles that God has performed because of His love. Though we are not worthy of anything, God still loves us, and it's because of this love that we remain to tell of His goodness.

ONE IN A MILLION FAITH | DAY 19

Without the Love of Christ, we wouldn't stand a chance to be healed, delivered, or set free. We would not have been the receiver of grace nor mercy. Love kept Christ focused on the plans and the assignment ahead of Him, the one that gave us hope. We are born into a sinful world, and it is the love of God that covers over a multitude of sins. Sickness sometimes can stem from choices we have made or it could be a generational curse; whatever the case may be, know that God's love will bring healing. God's love is unchanging and unfailing. He is the same today, yesterday, and forever more.

Heavenly Father, thank You for being unselfish; You allowed your son to die on the cross for the sake of Your creation. With Your love comes healing. Because of Your sacrifice of Your only begotten son, You gave me leniency and another chance at life when everything appeared so dim. Thank You for loving me throughout this journey filled with infirmities.

Question: When there is no greater love, how will you trust the love of God to cover you?

Christ Intercedes for Me

"Likewise the Spirit helps us in our weakness. For we do not know what to pray for as we ought, but the Spirit Himself intercedes for us with groanings too deep for words. 27 And he who searches hearts knows what is the mind of the Spirit, because the Spirit intercedes for the saints according to the will of God." (ESV)

ROMANS 8:26-27

He maketh Intercession for me. Sometimes our need is so great that we cannot find the words to express as we pray. That is when the Holy Spirit steps in and intercedes for us. He searches our hearts and our minds and sees what we need. Our Father already knows what we need before we ask or think, according to Romans 8:26-27. As the Spirit helps our infirmities, He knows what's best for us during prayer. When the words cannot flow forth from our mouths because our minds are filled with the problem and not the solution, Our Father has to intercede with groanings which cannot be uttered. When your body is in a lot of pain, you cannot help but to focus on the pain that is wracking your body. This comes with being a human; know that we have a God who intercedes and shall keep us in peace because we won't have to try and think about what will happen with our sickness or if our previous prayers will be heard. As the word states, we should pray without ceasing, but during those moments when words fail us, God will never fail us. He will never leave us

ONE IN A MILLION FAITH | DAY 20

nor forsake us. For He is Emmanuel, God is with us. I thank God for knowing each of us so well that he has the hairs on our heads numbered. With that said, Abba has all the words we need. He that searcheth the hearts knoweth the mind of the Spirit, because he maketh intercession. The Almighty Father knows what words are needed to move the heart of God on our behalf. This does not mean for us not to pray, but this reassures us that at the moment of lost words, God is interceding mightily for you and me.

I praise you today and always, and I thank You for being God. Father, I thank You for praying for me when I can't pray for myself. Sometimes, I just don't have the words to express my needs and desires to You. When I could not form the words in my mouth to pray and when the weight of the world rested heavily upon my shoulders, You made intercession to the Father on my behalf. Thank You for providing the Holy Spirit to help me when I am in need.

Question: Whom will you turn to for intercession when you are lost for words?

ONE IN A MILLION FAITH | DAY 21

Change of Garment

"And he, casting away his garment, rose, and came to Jesus." (KJV)

MARK 10:50

When Jesus is in the picture, responding to the cries of our afflictions, He always changes our garments and gives us a new identity. We are no longer recognized by the sickness, the brokenness, the lack, or any other circumstance that may have held us bound. When we are healed, our garment looks a lot more like Christ. As Jesus healed the blind man, he already knew that he was going to be given new garments, so he prepared in advance before reaching the Lord. The blind man did not want to be remembered with the old garments. God gives us an upgrade so that what we go through will not define us; it provides a testimony and a platform that lifts the Father and gives Him glory. God extends so many things when we allow Him to change our garments. We are filled with virtue, healing, strength, deliverance, freedom, and abundance as we allow God to have His way. The work that is started within us shall continue until it is completed according to scripture.

ONE IN A MILLION FAITH | DAY 21

Abba Father, thank You for responding to the cries of my affliction and healing my body. You have given me a change of garment so the world will know that You have healed me. No longer will I remain in the garment of a rare disease, but my garment of praise and garment of joy is quite fitting because of Your unfailing love.

Question: Which garment do you need to change?

ONE IN A MILLION FAITH | DAY 22

Prosperity

"Beloved, I wish above all things that you may prosper and be in health, even as your souls also prosper." (KJV)

III John 1:2

God's best is for us to prosper, and as we do, so we shall be in good health. The pains and the afflictions may come to flood our lives, but know that Jehovah wants the best for his children. The plan is for you to prosper and be in good health even as our souls prosper. Recognize that you are the beloved. Nothing can separate you from the love of God. The covenant that is made brings assurance that one day you will be healed. You will not only be healed, but your soul will prosper. God loves us so much He wants what is best for us. If you will allow yourself to take God out of the box, yield to His will, then the God of peace can do what He will in your life. The word requires a humbled and repenting heart for healing to take place. According to Isaiah 53:5, "But He was pierced for our transgressions; He was crushed for our iniquities; upon Him was the chastisement that brought us peace, and with His wounds we are healed." Jehovah-Rapha's love allowed Him to accept the call to want the best for us, so that everything that would take place would bring

ONE IN A MILLION FAITH | DAY 22

glory to the Father. No human being is ever willing to just allow another's pain of affliction to be upon them. I had to endure a series of surgeries, and I would not wish the pain alone upon another. The excruciating pain and the scars, no one would want to bear, but the God of our life bore it all upon the cross so that we could prosper and be in health.

God, I thank You for helping me recognize that You are in the midst of all situations. I praise You for when life seems unbearable. I give You thanks for times when life gets me down and I find it hard to see that You are doing a work that will allow me to prosper and be healed.

Question: Do you recognize the purpose of the affliction?

ONE IN A MILLION FAITH | DAY 23

Help Is On The Way

"My help comes from the Lord, the maker of heaven and earth." (GWT)

Psalm 121:2

His faithfulness is always assured. No matter what, God's words inform us of the many reasons we can trust God in peace. He has been faithful even before we were faithful to Him. He loved us even before we loved Him. As God remained faithful to the children of Israel, so shall He remain faithful to us. Whenever we cry out to God, He will help us. Whenever we are faced with daunting situations, we need to fall back on the truth of God's word. Reflect on the promises of God's words. We must give praise unto God, regardless of what we are going through. There were several times when I got down in self-pity that I couldn't muster up enough strength to give God praise. I had allowed my sickness to take control of me and muzzle my words of praise unto God. Never shall we allow the situation to stop us from giving God all glory and all praise. When you begin to praise, God is moved. The word of God tells us that we should enter into His gates with thanksgiving and praise. Take a look at Peter, when he was locked up in prison for doing nothing wrong, and when the angel of

ONE IN A MILLION FAITH | DAY 23

the Lord came to rescue and free Peter from a prison place, this is what our Heavenly Father does for us, He comes to free us from a place of sickness, the broken place, the lonely place. When we remind ourselves of God's goodness, it helps us endure the trials and tribulations of life because we know that help is on the way. In times of trouble, we need to turn to God and seek Him like never before.

Jehovah, I pray that You will comfort me in my suffering. I ask that You give skill to the hands of my doctors and bless the means used for my cure. Thank You for giving me the confidence in the power of Your grace, that even when I am afraid, I will trust You to be my help.

Question: What will you do as you wait for help?

ONE IN A MILLION FAITH | DAY 24

Gratitude

"Then one of them, when he saw that he was healed, turned back, praising God with a loud voice; 16 and he fell on his face at Jesus' feet, giving him thanks. Now he was a Samaritan." (ESV)

LUKE 17:15-16

The word of God teaches us that we must have a heart of gratitude. We are not deserving or worthy of anything because we have been born into a sinful world. When the almighty Healer shows Himself to be merciful and gracious unto us as He restores us back to wholeness, we must be thankful. This is not anything that we are owed. Jehovah heals those who are connected to the assignment and the plans of the mission already designed. Never in a million years would I have thought that I would have endured a rare disease that would nearly cost me my life. Understanding the importance of reverence unto God, understanding the importance of being allowed at another chance to move in purpose of God's assignment causes the heart to be moved. I woke up each day thanking God for every day that He allowed me to live through the afflictions. Though I was in pain, I was yet grateful that it was not the end. I believed that God was up to something in the midst of it all. The more I thanked God, the closer I got to my breakthrough for healing. I could begin to see

ONE IN A MILLION FAITH | DAY 24

the light at the end of the tunnel. Just as the one who turned back to give God praise and glorified him, when we show our gratitude, it makes God glad.

Father, thank You for bringing hope in the toughest of times, strengthening me for purpose. Thank You for the sacrifice to render healing to me, that hope was restored and faith was elevated. I give You thanks in all circumstances. Health is restored because of the one and true living Father.

Question: When you look at your situation, will you be the chosen one?

ONE IN A MILLION FAITH | DAY 25

A Discerning Mind

"Behold, I now do according to Your word. Behold, I give You a wise and discerning mind." (ESV)

I Kings 3:12

One of the many wonderful gifts the Father gives is that of a discerning spirit. We must come to realize that whatever situations we are faced with, maybe God is using the situation or the difficulty to do a work in us. Without providing for a time of healing and discernment, there will be no hope of living through this present moment without a shattering of our common life. We have to go through some things in life in order to grow. God gifts us with enough discernment to know, that regardless of what plan the enemy has, regardless of the situation, that God is with us. Discernment is knowing when to believe what a person speaks and when not to. While I was at a local hospital, the doctors told me that there was nothing else that they could do for me. The discernment had to kick in, and I began to pray and ask the Lord what my next steps were because I was not about to accept their words and go home and die. I told myself that I would live and not die. Many people, when they don't understand what God is doing, tend to give up, but I say to you, don't give

ONE IN A MILLION FAITH | DAY 25

up trusting God. Don't fight against what is taking place within you because of fear, lack of understanding, or hurt. Remain joyful through the situation and wait for God to turn your problems around while you are in the midst of the battle. Romans 8:28 tells us that all things will work together for our good. The sickness, the troubles at work, the divorce, none of these can direct God's plans. Have unconditional trust in God. You may remember Shadrach, Meshach, and Abednego, that allowed their trust to be unconditional so that as they were in the burning furnace, God was with them, and so He is with us in the midst of the battle.

Father, as Your word is rooted within, thank You for reminding me of Your word when I go through the fire. You held on to me so that I wouldn't give up. You allowed the gift of wisdom to rise when necessary. Thank You for being a present help in the time of trouble. God, You didn't give us the spirit of fear, but of power, love, and a sound mind to remain in peace no matter what circumstance is taking place.

Question: What mind will you allow to help you?

ONE IN A MILLION FAITH | DAY 26

Calling It Quits

"The LORD is my strength and my shield; my heart trusts in Him, and He helps me. My heart leaps for joy, and with my song I praise Him." (NIV)

Psalm 28:7

The more I trusted God in my weakness, the stronger I became, and the more I realized this truth: I am nothing without God. I could not heal myself and neither could the doctors heal me without the help of God. He provides the power and help to accomplish the assignment. In this case, it was the assignment of healing through the hands of the surgeons. The more we go through situations, we realize how much more we need God. We are ready to give up and quit when things become overwhelming. I love that Moses wasn't afraid to admit his weaknesses to God. As Moses found out God was his help and strength, I had to find that out every time my lungs collapsed and I was unable to breathe on my own. Quitting would have meant that I had given the enemy the upper hand. However, trusting in God's truths provided strength each time, and He never failed me. Every time my lung would not expand and the staff would bring in another chest tube, I called on Jehovah to breathe through my lungs and that they would inflate so that I could breathe. Every time

Question: How much does it mean to you to live again?

ONE IN A MILLION FAITH | DAY 27

The Lonely State

"... I will never leave you nor forsake you."
(KJV)

Hebrews 13:5

If God's not moving at your rate of speed, you must still trust God. Time cannot be redeemed, so we must not waste it. As time ticks away, there are several things that take place. There are lessons to be learned, plans to be established, assignments to be completed, healing to take place, and restoration to be had. As the children of Israel walked in the wilderness, a three-day journey turned into a 40-year journey. Throughout this journey, many of the Israelites felt alone and abandoned, but God was with them. This is how I felt during my illness. I felt as if no one was there to go through this journey with me. I started to grow sad, feeling as if no one in the world understood what I was going through. The enemy started to attack my mind with thoughts of negativity, doubt, and depression. My train of thought was starting to yield over to the enemy. As I was growing up, I used to always hear people use the phrase, "An idle mind is the enemy's camp." Well, I realized that for the amount of time that I was admitted into the hospital, my thoughts had to fight to align with

ONE IN A MILLION FAITH | DAY 27

the positive thoughts. When the enemy comes to battle with our minds, we have to operate with the Mind of Christ and remain strong, not allowing ourselves to be enslaved to the attacks of the mind. Avoiding those fiery darts that the enemy throws to make us battle becomes hard if we are not anchored in Christ. Stay grounded, stay anchored. Don't be in a rush to exit God's timing. I gained patience and wisdom through God's timing.

I thank You, Father, for being a promise keeper. You never left me nor forsook me as I went through a period of affliction, not knowing whether I was going to live or die. Thank you for not allowing Your word to return void. Thank You for loving me while I went into the valley.

Question: What will you gain as you wait on God's timing?

ONE IN A MILLION FAITH | DAY 28

You Got The Victory

"But thanks be to God, which giveth us the victory through our Lord Jesus Christ."
(KJV)

1 CORINTHIANS 15:57

I am thankful that Jesus died on the cross so that we may live and have the victory over those things that come into our lives to take us out. John 10:10 lets us know that the enemy comes to steal, kill, and destroy, while the giver of life came so that we may have life and have it more abundantly. It is not God's intention to create us without purpose. Everything that we go through has purpose, especially those mundane trials and tribulations, sicknesses, and warfare -- they all serve a purpose. We must know that there is victory at the end of the trials we face if we hold on to God's unchanging hands. It is only because of the Father that we are kept here on earth to share the story. No one can tell a testimony the way that they would if they have not experienced all that they were dealt. The cards appear to be unfair as you go through the trials; however, when you reach the end, climb out of the valley and get to the top of the mountain; the victory belongs to you. As I was dealing with catamenial pneumothorax and hemothorax, I was reminded by the Holy Spirit that the sickness was not going to take me out. This was a testament in the making, to help someone else. That is easier said than done, now

ONE IN A MILLION FAITH | DAY 28

that I have achieved the victory. When we take the focus from the sickness, the lack, the grief, the divorce, and ourselves, we can see the victory. We must speak the victory before it happens. We must encourage ourselves daily, and the situation is conquered. I would remind myself that I was in a temporary state and my physical body would not always be with sickness, but one day I would be totally healed. The day that I was able to make other plans and not have to worry about going to a doctor appointment was amazing. It felt like a burden was lifted from me. The weight of the world was no longer on my shoulders. I felt as though I had achieved the right to embrace the healing. My Father had set me free from the chains and bondage of sickness. You shall smile again. Stay positive, keep believing, keep speaking victory, because the victory belongs to you.

God, You are so faithful. As You responded to Martha and answered her cries, I thank You for responding to my cries of affliction, too. Thank you, Father, for not allowing this sickness to be unto death, but using it to bring You glory. Thank You, Lord, for I know that victory comes only because of Your grace and mercy.

Question: Are you ready to receive the victory that God has for you?

Refuge

"In the fear of the Lord there is strong confidence, and his children will have refuge."
(KJV)

Proverbs 14:26

When you look at the children of Israel going through each day, guided by the clouds during the day and led by the fire at night, it should encourage your Spirit. The hardship of my health crisis required me to seek God's heart, his bosom for a place of refuge. As the Lord hides us in the shadow of the almighty, we must continue walking in His love. When we are in the dark valley, we shall fear no evil as Psalm 23 reminds us of. Knowing that we have a safe place to rest when the pressures of life try to consume us, we should look to Jesus to be the safe haven. God is Elohim, our strength and our peace. We will not be moved by the enemy trying to steal our joy or peace; it doesn't belong to him. God created us with purpose and His purpose shall be manifested for God to get the glory and the honor. This day belongs to God. We belong to God. We shall live and not die, because according to Psalm 71:3, we can continually come to the rock of habitation... for God is our rock and our fortress. The price has been paid on the cross. So, let your first response to every disappointment and every challenge be to seek refuge in Christ

that I had to go under the knife, I needed the shield that only God could provide -- that shield of protection, the blood that covered me, so that I would survive. I sing praise unto my God for saving my life. One in a Million Lives for another chance.

Father, You are the giver of life. As You renew our hearts and minds and save our souls, I thank You for the gift of life being redeemed. I praise You for performing a miracle and displaying it through Your people. You allow the air that You breathed to flow through my lungs that I would be kept to tell of Your goodness.

ONE IN A MILLION FAITH | DAY 29

Jesus. Purposefully press into the righteousness, peace, and joy that is in God's kingdom. God is bringing us to a place where everything we say and do becomes as effective as if He said it or did it. Let My peace act as the umpire in your heart, settling with finality every controversy, every expectation, says God. Jehovah will not allow us to be brought to shame because we dared to hope and dared to believe for better things. God is a God of renewed opportunity, even where failure or sickness has dominated before. Fear not but believe only, and you will see of the travail of your soul and be satisfied. Seek refuge in the only true and living God who can protect us and get us to the victory.

Father, You have made me in the likeness of Your image. Thank You for building confidence within me that I may be able to withstand the fiery darts thrown by the enemy to take me out of the good fight. Thank You for the strength to stand while in the dark places, knowing that You are with me wherever I go. I will not make it without Your leading of the Holy Spirit. With You I can do the impossible. I take refuge as You hide me in your bosom and protect me from the snare and the wiles of the enemy.

Question: Where will you seek refuge?

ONE IN A MILLION FAITH | DAY 30

Do Not Lose Heart

"Therefore we don't faint, but though our outward person is decaying, yet our inward person is renewed day by day (WEB)"

2 CORINTHIANS 4:16

During my affliction, I had to realize that strength and faith needed each other in order for me to be healed. Understanding that my strength came from the Father, I would stand regardless of what my body was going through. According to scripture, "For our light affliction, which is for the moment, works for us more and more exceedingly an eternal weight of glory". Know that you are in Jehovah's glory during the affliction. Though the body may be weak, God is doing a work on the inward parts so that it is renewed. We must not only look at the things that we can see, but look at that which we cannot see and stand on faith, not losing heart. Scripture tells me in Corinthians 4:18, those things which are seen are temporal, but the things which are not seen are eternal. While you operate in faith, do not lose heart. Don't focus on the things that come against you or are able to bring you down. Don't let your affliction dictate your behavior. Focus on the finished work, look ahead to the promises of Christ; trusting that He has worked healing and deliverance out in the supernatural;

waiting on the season that manifestation will spring forth into the natural, so all can see the healing and deliverance in your life.

Father, as the enemy's plan is to frustrate my faith, I thank you for giving the eyes to see beyond to my promise. Abba Father, you are the healer and a restorer of that which is broken, afflicted or damaged. Thank you for keeping me focused on you and not my issue.

Question: Sometimes our issues can discourage us from seeing the promise. What is causing you to lose heart and hindering you from focusing on the promises of God for the victory?

ABOUT THE AUTHOR

Tamekia Green-Judge is devout Christian who does not mind sharing her faith. She is a member of Love House Ministries, where the pastor is Apostle Randy Roberts and the senior pastor is Theresa Roberts. She gave her life to the Lord in May 2003 while attending Church of the Harvest Ministries, located in St. Helena, S.C. She then began to grow and do the work of the Lord.

During her walk with Christ, she has been used to help many people by allowing God's spiritual gifts to flow through her. God has given her an eye to assist individuals as they go through everyday life, dealing with the many situations they face. She's an intercessor, finance officer, director of records management, seasonal tax preparer, soccer mom, and an upcoming author. She can often be found helping others establish businesses as she shares the word of God. She is also the co-founder of Cam Cam Enterprises, LLC and Cam Cam Tire Repair Services, LLC. Tamekia resides in Beaufort, S.C., with her husband, James, son Cameron, and their precious fur ball, Munchkin.

In 2009, Tamekia was diagnosed with a rare medical condition that nearly caused her to succumb to the disease. Her faith helped her to overcome the health challenges, giving her a will to live through her trials, as she became a living testimony, a miracle saved by grace.

In 1998, Tamekia obtained a certificate in small business, a certificate in general education, and an associate of arts degree in general business from the Technical College of the Lowcountry, Beaufort, S.C. The following year, she continued her education and pursued a bachelor's degree in business management from Park University, Parkville, Mo., and in 2004 she graduated with a master's degree in business administration, and she utilizes her knowledge and the skills to help others.

www.ingramcontent.com/pod-product-compliance
Lightning Source LLC
Chambersburg PA
CBHW070905080526
44589CB00013B/1189